SERVING ON A JURY

A TRUE BOOK

by

Sarah De Capua

Children's Press®
A Division of Scholastic Inc.

New York Toronto London Auckland Sydney
Mexico City New Delhi Hong Kong
Danbury, Connecticut

A lawyer questioning a witness during a jury trial

Reading Consultant
Nanci R. Vargus, Ed.D.
Teacher in Residence
University of Indianapolis
Indianapolis, Indiana

Content Consultant
Donald S. White, J.D.

Dedication:
To Conner

The photograph on the cover shows a lawyer presenting a case to a jury. The photograph on the title page shows a jury foreman reading a verdict.

Library of Congress Cataloging-in-Publication Data

Sarah De Capua.
    Serving on a Jury / by Sarah De Capua.
        p. cm. — (A True book)
    Includes bibliographical references and index.
    ISBN 0-516-22329-1 (lib.bdg.)   0-516-27364-7 (pbk.)
    1. Jury—United States—Juvenile literature. [1. Jury.] I. Title.
II. Series.
KF8972.Z9 D38   2002
347.73'52—dc21   00-047365

©2002 Children's Press®
A Division of Scholastic Inc.
All rights reserved. Published simultaneously in Canada.
Printed in China.

6 7 8 9 10 R 11 10 09 08 07

Contents

A courtroom during a trial

What Is a Jury?

Do you know anyone who has served on a jury? Have you seen television programs that feature juries? Perhaps you have heard news reports about real-life trials and the decisions made by juries.

A trial jury is a group of people who listen to the facts

Serving on a jury is an important responsibility.

of a case and decide whether the person accused of a crime is guilty or not guilty. People who serve on a jury are called jurors. When they serve, they carry on one of the important traditions on which the United States was founded.

Trial by jury began in ancient Greece about 400 B.C. At that time, juries were made up of between 201 and 1,001 members. A set of rules made sure jurors were chosen fairly. One of the rules said that only honest citizens who would take their roles as jurors seriously could serve. This rule is still important for present-day jurors.

In Greece, the decision of the jury, called the verdict (VER-dikt), was decided by a secret ballot. Secret ballots are votes that are cast without anyone knowing how any other juror voted. Then the votes were counted. The verdict was the decision that received the most votes.

England began the practice of trial by jury in 1066. English colonists brought the jury system

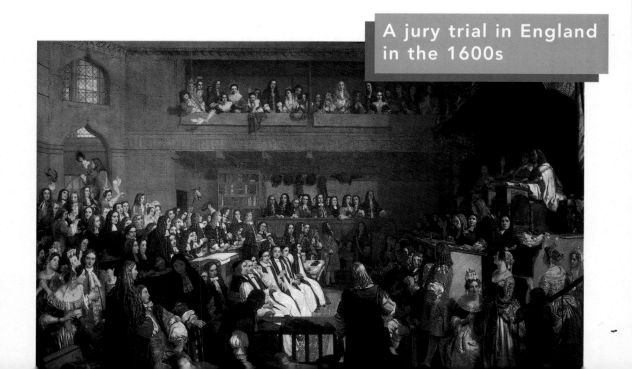

A jury trial in England in the 1600s

A jury trial in New York in the 1730s

with them to North America in the 1600s. The colonies became the United States of America in 1776. By then, trial by jury was already an important part of justice in most of the original thirteen states.

The U.S. Constitution guarantees that any person who has been accused of a crime has the right to a trial by jury.

Today, the right to a trial by jury is guaranteed by the U.S. Constitution. The U.S. Constitution is the document containing the principles that govern the United States. All fifty U.S. state constitutions also guarantee a person's right to trial by jury.

Two Kinds of Trials

You're probably most familiar with criminal trials. These trials involve a person who has been accused of a crime, such as robbery or murder. The punishment for a person found guilty in a criminal trial may be a fine, community service, prison, or death.

A police officer talking about evidence at a criminal trial

The second kind of trial is a civil trial. These trials involve disputes between people. Such a dispute is called a lawsuit. For example, a person injured in a car accident might bring a lawsuit against the person he or she claims caused the accident. In a civil jury trial, the punishment usually involves paying the wronged person or people a sum of money.

A lawyer questioning a witness during a civil trial

Who Can Serve on a Jury?

In most places in the United States, anyone who is a U.S. citizen, is at least eighteen years old, is able to understand English, and has stayed out of serious trouble with the law can serve on a jury. However, state and national laws have other requirements

12

Anyone who is at least eighteen years old, is a U.S. citizen, and has not committed a serious crime may be asked to serve on a jury.

that may have to be met before a person can serve as a juror.

Today, computers are used to decide who can serve on a jury. Using driver's-license and voter-registration files, the computer searches for the names of all the people in the community who meet the requirements for jury service. The computer first picks the names of people who have never served on a jury. It then searches through the names of people who have already served on a jury. The computer is programmed to pick people whose last jury service was a long time ago.

A jury-duty notice

People who are chosen for jury duty receive a notice in the mail. The notice states a date, time, and place the person should appear. The date is usually about a month away. The time is likely to be in the morning, about 8 or 9A.M.

A county courthouse in Texas

The place is almost always a local courthouse.

The notice also provides space for a person to explain why he or she cannot perform jury duty. Reasons may include a long illness, a problem with a person's vision or hearing, or a demanding job. The juror must provide the explanation and mail the notice back to the courthouse. The court usually accepts the juror's reason and excuses that person from jury duty. However, in most cases, a juror cannot be excused from jury duty forever. He or she will receive another notice some months or years later. At that time, the person will be expected to serve.

Selecting the Jury

Receiving a jury-duty notice does not mean a person will definitely serve on a jury. On the day of a trial as many as three hundred people may be called to the courthouse. Everyone reports to a waiting room. After a while, a court

Hundreds of people may be called in at the beginning of the jury-selection process.

A court officer reads off the names of people to be considered as jurors.

officer appears and reads aloud the names of about twenty to thirty people who have been chosen at random. The names the officer reads aloud are one step closer to serving on the jury.

The next step takes place inside the courtroom. The people whose names were chosen go into the courtroom where the trial is scheduled to take place. The judge and lawyers for the case are there too. The

A courtroom during jury selection

judge is the person who listens to cases and decides what evidence will be heard. The lawyers speak for the two sides arguing the case.

One or more lawyers represent the plaintiff (PLAYN-tif)—the side that has been wronged. In a criminal trial, the plaintiff is the city, county, or state where the crime took place. This is because a crime is considered an act against society. In a civil trial, the plaintiff is the person or people bringing the lawsuit.

The other side is made up of one or more lawyers who represent the defendant (di-FEN-duhnt)—the person or people accused of wrongdoing. In a criminal trial, the defendant is the person who has been accused of a crime. In a civil trial, the defendant is the person or people being sued.

The jurors listen as the judge describes the facts of the case.

These facts include the charges against the defendant and the time and place the crime or event occurred. The judge then tells the jurors how long the trial is expected to last. A trial may be completed in one day, or it may take weeks or even months.

When the judge has finished speaking, the lawyers for both sides ask each juror a few questions. Sometimes the judge asks questions too. The questions are designed to make sure that a juror will be fair and open-minded. Lawyers for both sides want

A lawyer for the plaintiff (above) and a lawyer for the defendant (left) question possible jurors during jury selection.

to be certain that a juror won't decide the case in his or her mind before the juror knows all the evidence in the case.

During this questioning, which can take several hours, many people are excused from jury duty. After all the jurors (usually twelve) and some alternates have been selected, the questioning is completed. An alternate is an extra juror. Alternates serve if a juror cannot continue jury duty because of illness or some other sudden event that occurs during the trial. The jury is now ready to do its important work.

What Does a Jury Do?

In a criminal trial, the jury decides whether the person accused of a crime is guilty. If the defendant is found guilty, the jury sometimes suggests how he or she should be punished. In most cases, however, the judge decides the punishment.

Jurors are sworn in, or take an oath to be fair, at the beginning of a trial.

In a civil trial, the jury decides who has won the lawsuit—the plaintiff or the defendant. If the jury decides in favor of the

A jury trial in session

plaintiff, it also decides how much money the defendant has to pay the plaintiff.

During the trial, the lawyer for the plaintiff (called the prosecutor) and the lawyer for the

During a trial, the jury listens as the prosecutor (above) and the defense attorney (right) question witnesses.

defendant take turns presenting evidence to support their
case. Members of the jury listen
carefully to all the evidence.

Jurors are not allowed to talk about the case with one another or with family members or friends. A juror who breaks this rule may be dismissed from jury duty. Sometimes, breaking this rule means that a new trial, with all new jurors, must be held.

If a trial lasts for more than one day, jurors usually are allowed to go home when the judge dismisses the court for the day. This occurs about 4 or 5 P.M. Jurors return to court the following day and the trial continues.

During some trials, however, jurors are not allowed to go home. This is called being sequestered (suh-KWEST-erd). Judges may sequester jurors during criminal trials concerning serious crimes, such as murder. Jurors may also be sequestered during cases that are being reported on by many newspapers and television news programs. In such cases, jurors are taken to a hotel where they stay every night until the trial ends. At the hotel, jurors are not allowed to read magazines or newspapers, or watch television. This keeps the jurors from being influenced by reporters.

A juror's most important job is to remain fair. Jurors

A juror must listen to all the evidence before making a decision about the case.

should not develop an opinion about a case until all the facts have been heard.

Reaching a Verdict

After the lawyers for the plaintiff and defendant have presented their evidence, the jury must decide which side they should rule in favor of. This is called "reaching a verdict."

The judge instructs all the jurors, except the alternates, to go to another room in the

Jurors decide on verdicts in jury rooms like the one above.

courthouse. This jury room
contains a long table and a
chair for each juror. There, the

jurors will finally be able to talk about the case. They review all the evidence. Then they vote. In a criminal trial, they vote "guilty" or "not guilty." In a civil trial, the jury votes for the plaintiff or the defendant. In most cases, the verdict in a criminal case must be unanimous. This means that all the members of the jury must agree. In a civil case, usually at least nine of the twelve jurors must agree on the verdict.

All juries have a leader, known as a foreperson. This man or woman leads the discussion and counts the jurors' votes. Leading the jurors can be a difficult job. Sometimes they don't agree with one another. They may argue and yell at each other because they want the jury to vote a certain way. The leader must keep everyone calm and focused on their duty.

A jury may discuss a verdict for a few hours, or for several days. If a jury needs more than a few hours to reach a verdict, they may leave the jury room and come back the next day.

It can be difficult to reach a unanimous decision. Sometimes, even after working very hard, a jury cannot agree on a verdict. The foreperson then reports this fact to the judge. A jury that does not reach a verdict is called a hung jury. When this happens, a new trial must take place, with a new jury.

A jury forewoman reading a verdict aloud to the court

Most juries do reach a verdict, however. The foreperson sends a message to the judge that the jury is ready to announce its decision. The judge, jury, lawyers, plaintiff, and defendant come back to the courtroom. In some places, the foreperson reads the verdict aloud. In other places, the foreperson gives the verdict to the judge, and the court clerk reads the verdict.

Soon after, the judge thanks the jurors for their service and dismisses them. Once their jury duty is complete, jurors are allowed to discuss the case with anyone.

No matter what type of trial a juror participates in, he or she should feel privileged to

A juror is interviewed by reporters after a trial.

have performed an important community service. Jury duty is one of many ways to be a good citizen.

To Find Out More

Here are some additional resources to help you learn more about serving on a jury:

 **Books**

De Capua, Sarah. **Becoming a Citizen.** Children's Press, 2002.

De Capua, Sarah. **Voting.** Children's Press, 2002.

Kerr, Daisy. **Ancient Greeks.** Franklin Watts, 1997.

Miller, Marvin. **You Be the Jury.** Scholastic, 1992.

Quiri, Patricia Ryon. **The Constitution.** Children's Press, 1998.

Organizations and Online Sites

The Juror's Web Site

http://www.members. tripod.com/~jctmac/

This site provides easy-to-understand information about jury duty. It explains how a trial works and includes links to other jury-related sites.

Jury Duty

Go to any World Wide Web search engine and type "jury duty." You will get a list by state of the different types of courts. You can then choose the court in your state that you want to learn more about. Included are rules for trials and jurors.

National Center for State Courts

http://www.ncsc.dni.us

300 Newport Avenue
Williamsburg, VA 23185

The NCSC is an information resource for lawyers, courts, and juries. Includes publications and reports available to the public, and links to other sites.

Important Words

accuse to charge a person with wrongdoing

colonists people who live in a newly settled area

dismiss to allow a person to leave

dispute argument

evidence information and facts that help prove something

guilty having done something wrong

justice the system of laws and judgment in a country

principles rules of conduct

sue to start a case against someone in a court of law

tradition the handing down of customs, ideas, and beliefs from one generation to the next

trial the examination of evidence in a court of law to decide if a charge or claim is true

Index

Meet the Author

Sarah De Capua received her master of arts in teaching degree in 1993 and has since been educating children, first as a teacher and currently as an editor and author of children's books. Other books she has written for Children's Press include *Becoming a Citizen*, *Paying Taxes*, *Running for Public Office*, and *Voting* (True Books); *J.C. Watts, Jr.: Character Counts* (Community Builders); and several titles in the Rookie Read-About® Geography series.

Ms. De Capua resides in Colorado.